Self–Publishing on Amazon with Ease

'Dotun Owolabi

ISBN: 9798745424083

Contents

DEDICATION

INTRODUCTION

I want you to visualize a stormy winter night in a secluded cabin, on a forlorn and deserted Island, where there was no electric connection to power the warmer or heater. What will you do with the smoldering pieces of log of wood alongside others that are still available?

You will want to kindle every available log of wood because if the spark goes out, the consequences may be deadly. Anyone in that context can even freeze to death.

Ideas are the stimulant and assets of every Civilization. In other words, ideas rule the world. But the fundamental challenges readily faced by the 'inspired' or the 'inventor', in most cases, is their inability or incompetence to transmit and preserve their ingenuity into concrete concepts that are accessible readily. If their superb ideas are missing, what will the emerging generation build on?

An Oriental Proverb quip 'The best memory is weaker than the faintest pen'. Ideas and inspiration not captured instantly stand a chance of being lost permanently. On the flip side, if it is documented, it is of no use if not communicated and published for the world to read.

Interestingly, traditional Publishers no longer hold the aces. They do not have a say if your voice in print will be heard or not. We believe Traditional Publishers have been a veritable platform for Authors the World over. However, times and seasons have changed and many of them that do not follow through with the trend of time will be lost in transition.

Traditional Publishing Firms now use the emergence of their Authors on Amazon's best-selling list as a bragging right and certification. That simply means, ignoring Amazon and Kindle Publishing Platform to your jeopardy. Therefore, rather than go through the traditional route, it is better to stay with Amazon and learn the rudiments of how to publish on Kindle with ease.

Self-publishing is not rocket science and it is not 'Hard Maths' for those who detest 'Calculus. The primary purpose of this book is to demystify Self-Publishing, on Amazon and encourage writers to go ahead and share their passion or idea with zeal and zest. You can create and complete that book. Yes, you can.

Why write?

If you are still contemplating and speculating, please note this ancient African Proverb about writing that quip: 'Until the Lion knows how to write, every story will glorify the Hunter'.

This presupposes the fact that no one can tell your story better than you. No one will be able to analyze and depict your burden, passion, and solutions like you. Nobody will ever come close. No one was born a writer. We all grow into writing after years of deliberate commitment to reading, observing, and deducing. It's commonly said that readers are leaders. I believe as well readers are writers. If you don't read, you will not be able to be a prolific writer. That's why I'm convinced that the platform Amazon has afforded everyone – Readers and Writers as well as content creators – should not be wasted.

Reedys blog highlights practical steps to writing a book:

The steps listed are achievable with a laser-like focus. The Blog quotes "To help you achieve just that, we've put together this 15-step guide to how to write a book, chock full of information and advice from the most prolific, successful writers in the business. Whether you've been an aspiring author since your childhood or five minutes ago, this article will give you all the knowledge you need to write a book and do it well.

- Find your "big idea"

- Research your genre

- Create an outline

- Start strong

- Focus on substance

- Write "reader-first"

- Set word count goals

- Establish a healthy routine

- Set up a productive space

- Use writing software

- Keep yourself motivated

- Take setbacks as they come

- Don't rush the ending

- Get tons of feedback

- Publish your book

The Blog posited 'For many people, writing a book has been a lifelong dream, yet one that's always seemed just out of reach. Indeed, as we reveal in our publishing podcast Bestseller, roughly 80% of Americans have wanted to write and publish a book at some point — but less than 0.1% have done it. Now that's appalling on the premise of those who successfully published as against those who still wish to. The disparity is enormous and frightening.

The Writers of the blog stated "For many people, writing a book has been a lifelong dream, yet one that's always seemed just out of reach. Indeed, as we reveal in our publishing podcast Bestseller, roughly 80% of Americans have wanted to write and publish a book at some point — but fewer than 0.1% have done it". The disparity between those who dream about writing and those who write is appalling.

Remarkably, Jeff Goins wrote 'The hard part of writing a book isn't getting published. It is the actual writing'. In his article captioned '10 Ridiculously Simple Steps for Writing a Book', Jeff

Goins highlighted vital steps to take to creatively write a book:

i. Decide what the book is about
ii. Set a daily word count goal
iii. Set a time to work on your book every day
iv. Write in the same place every time
v. Set a total word count
vi. Give yourself weekly deadlines
vii. Get early feedback
viii. Commit to shipping
ix. Embrace failure
x. Write another book

He further gave 10 more writing tips:

- Only write one chapter at a time
- Write a shorter book
- Start a blog to get feedback early
- Keep an inspiration list
- Keep a journal
- Deliver consistently
- Take frequent breaks
- Remove distractions
- Write where others are writing (or working)
- Don't edit as you go

What's Amazon Kindle?

According to Wikipedia 'Amazon Kindle is a series of e-readers designed and marketed by Amazon. Amazon Kindle devices enable users to browse, buy, download, and read e-books, newspapers, magazines, and other digital media via wireless networking to the Kindle Store'.

In 2004, Amazon founder and CEO Jeff Bezos instructed the company's employees to build the world's best e-reader before Amazon's competitors could. Amazon originally used the Codename Fiona for the device.

Branding consultants Michael Cronan and Karin Hibma devised the 'Kindle' name. Lab126 asked them to name the product, and they suggested "kindle", meaning to light a fire. They felt this was an apt metaphor for reading and intellectual excitement.

According to Wikipedia 'Amazon released the Kindle, its first e-reader on November 19, 2007, for $399. It sold out in 5 1/2 hours. The device remained out of stock for five months until late April 2008'.

Other Kindle devices had been released since then till as late as March 2019. About its features, Wikipedia states "Kindle devices support dictionary and Wikipedia look-up functions when highlighting a word in an e-book. The font type, size, and margins can be customized. Kindles are charged by connecting to a computer's USB port or an AC adapter. Users needing accessibility due to impaired vision can use an audio adapter to listen to any e-book read aloud on supported Kindles, or those with difficulty in reading the text may use the Amazon Ember Bold font for darker text and other fonts may too have bold font versions."

The emergence of the e-readers' platform that is dominated by Amazon kindle changed the paradigm of reading, researching, studying, and information exchange forever. Amazon Kindle was the game changer and it's still the pacesetter today. It is worthy of note for every aspiring Writer and Author that are tired of the racketeering and complexities of Traditional Publishing to give Kindle a shot. It is going to be worth it.

CHAPTER 1
TRADITIONAL PUBLISHING VERSUS SELF-PUBLISHING

Traditional Publishing is the status–quo way of reeling out books where an Author engages the services of an agent who will negotiate with the publishers to ensure the publication of the Writer's manuscript. Alternatively, you may submit a query letter/proposal with your manuscript and upon scrutiny by the publisher's Editor, they will decide to publish your work or not.

According to Masterclass.com, "Traditional publishing means that your book is published by an established publishing house (often based in New York), with a team of professional people to take care of the book design, sales, marketing, and various other processes of the publishing world".

It is affirmed on the website that Traditional Publishers don't accept manuscripts directly from Writers but only from Literary Agents. This as it were, takes a lot of processing. It might even take years to get your work published and get in the hands of the eventual readers.

However, the edge that comes with Traditional Publishing is enviable in some cases. You have a team of professionals in place, with an established platform to sell your work and you stand a greater chance of not spending a dine to get everything done – no overhead cost.

On the flip side, we look at Self – Publishing. Masterclass website avers "Self-publishing is when an author decides to print and distribute their work themselves—usually through a self-publishing platform—bypassing traditional publishing companies. Self-publishing provides you with the ultimate freedom and control over your creative work".

The advantages of these are that you are your boss, you get much more profit and the publishing of your manuscript is guaranteed. The idea gets shared immediately. If the publication becomes a success, you cut out middlemen and smile to the bank extravagantly.

But are there shortcomings to these two means of publishing? Definitely yes. Starting with

Traditional Publishing, we discover that its process is incredibly slow. Getting a literary agent can take more than a year and the process with the Publishers itself is not exceptionally fast. Moreover, by signing a contract, you might lose creative control over your work and future choices. The Royalty you get from Traditional Publishers will be very low because they think they are helping you and have incurred so much cost because of trying to give you a platform.

The disadvantages traceable to Self – Publishing are also many-sided. You are the one to engage all the professionals at your cost. The other challenge is the fact that there is no platform for you to ride on. No prestige, validation, approval, or recommendation. No one will vouch for your pedigree.

The Creative Penn website avers "You need a budget upfront if you want a professional result. These days, you're likely to spend on professional editing before submitting to an agent anyway, or at least be spending on books and courses for writers. Everyone spends money on their hobby, so whether you're knitting or writing or mountain biking, most people are happy to spend money they never get back on something they love. However, if like me, you're intending to make a living from this, then yes, you need to invest money in creating intellectual property assets for the business to get it back in multiple streams of income".

This implies the fact that you need a substantial amount of capital to fund the Publication process if you are self – Publishing. Therefore, the strength of your pocket might ultimately determine how well your book will sell in the market.

Having seen the incredible advantage of Self – Publishing, I will submit to the fact that it has changed the paradigm of Publishing, especially since the advent of the internet and it will continue to give emerging authors and writers a voice that will not be taken to the grave.

I will conclude with what Bella Rose Pope said on self – The publishing Website thus: "However, self-publishing gives you an alternative path. It gives you an assured chance of getting your book out there. You have a better chance of seeing success in your sales and making an impact if your message resonates with enough people. Not to mention, you get to stay true to the vision of your book. Self-publishing allows you the freedom, money, community, and control to shape your life into one that you adore. So, start writing your bestseller today".

There is a book in you and we can't wait to read and be inspired, challenged, entertained, motivated, and changed.

CHAPTER 2
DETAILS OF AMAZON'S KINDLE

Kindle Direct Distributing (KDP) is Amazon's book distributing platform that can be utilized to independently publish a book on the web, which readers can buy as a digital book/eBook or print-on-request book. It is one of the top self-publishing organizations and at the moment leads the independent publishing book marketplace.

Amazon KDP is a key part of the distributing business, right now holding something like 80% of the digital-book market.

On account of Amazon KDP's start off in 2007, present-day essayists and researchers are confronted with a significant choice when deciding how to turn into a writer.

Journalists of all disciplines have partaken in a blast in professional adaptability throughout the past ten years or so with ascend in remote composing positions. This flare has prompted the expansion in distributing digital books, print books, and more through independently publishing.

Writers have two options for distributing their books: conventional publishing or independent publishing. While gauging the conventional distributing versus independently publishing choices, numerous essayists consider the higher eminence rates on KDP, and the simplicity of independently publishing, as there are no cutthroat circles to go through like there is with customary distributing.

KDP Publishing is an exceptional platform for writers to independently publish digital books and soft cover books.

For digital books, writers can readily transmit their books and documents, and it will be accessed in the Kindle Store as a digital book for readers to buy and instantly download.

For printed books, writers transfer their book records and KDP Distributing utilizes print-on-request innovation to print the soft cover book whenever it's bought; the printing costs will be deducted from the royalties you obtain from each book sold.

KDP Publishing Methodology:

• Transfer your book details or content to Amazon KDP.

• Publish on the KDP Platform.

• The reader could buy your digital book instantly and transfer it to their device.

• Readers can opt for the soft cover copy of your book and Amazon's KDP platform will employ print-on-request innovation to print and deliver your book directly to the reader once bought.

• Amazon will pay you book royalties per book sold on the KDP stage.

Why opt for Amazon KDP amongst others?

There are innumerable advantages and advantages to self-publishing your book on the KDP Platform. The Amazon KDP Distributing stage has reformed the Publishing business tremendously and innovatively, by offering writers the chance to make it simpler to distribute a book and make a manageable book business.

These are the advantages of KDP Distributing:

Wide Spread and Coverage. Amazon's footing is immense, and that implies creators can take advantage of worldwide business sectors across the US, Europe, Asia, and Africa.

Improved Royalties. With Amazon, creators/authors can procure higher royalty rates than they regularly would through normal Publishing houses. Contingent upon the sort of book you sell on Amazon, Royalty rates can be just about as high as a whopping 60%. Now, that's unprecedented.

Creator privileges/rights. Even though you distribute your book to KDP, you hold the privileges to your book through Amazon's non-restrictive arrangement.

Speedy Publishing time. Commonly, with Conventional Publishers, books can consume a large chunk of the day to get to the store or buyer. But with Amazon's innovation and dexterity, the KDP distributing process is exceptionally prompt and extremely speedy.

No stock. A distant memory is the days when writers needed to buy printed duplicates of books upfront to sell them. With print-on-request innovation and KDP's revolution, books are printed as they are bought. That's impressive and a huge relief to Authors and Creators.

Amazon's Kindle Publication Rate and Royalties

Ideally, Publishing on Amazon's Kindle should be on the high side with expenses not easily affordable by aspiring Authors/Creators on the premise of its innovation and seamless means of transmitting ideas and creativity.

Consequently, what amount does it cost to independently publish on Amazon KDP?

Publishing a book on Amazon KDP is free. It doesn't cost creators anything initially. In any case, if you are selling soft cover books on Amazon, the expense to print the book will be deducted by Amazon from your book Royalties. This implies that when you sell a soft cover book, you will pay for the cost to print the book.

KDP's Royalties Methodology

Amazon's Kindle Direct Publishing Authors are primarily paid via Royalties dues. The Royalties are not the same for the eBook and the Paperback.

The Royalty rate for digital books is 35% or 70%, contingent upon which Royalty rate your book is qualified for.

The Royalty rate for soft cover books is a decent 60% fixed rate.

KDP pays roughly 60 days after the month's end that your Royalty was accrued

Notwithstanding, a proviso to this is that your installment sum should meet a base limit before it is paid out. You can decide to be paid out through a few choices including wire transfer, cheque, or direct deposit.

What is KDP Select?

KDP Select is a program for writers to give Amazon exclusive permission to sell a digital book on just Amazon's Kindle and nowhere else. This implies that the writer's digital book can only be accessed on Amazon's Kindle stage, and the writer can't utilize another self-publishing means to circulate their digital book/eBook. The exclusive rights have some benefits that include: Promotional tools and wherein possible higher Royalties Rates.

However, if you're thinking about signing up for KDP Select, your enlistment isn't endless, meaning you can test it out for 90 days. KDP Select enlistment goes on for 90 days, which permits creators the choice to auto-renew their enlistment in KDP Select for an additional 90 days, or quit.

CHAPTER 3
EBOOK'S EDGE

If this were to be a law court. I would pick you as the Judge and the Jury. The plaintiff is Traditional Publishing while the Defendant is Self–Publishing. Self–Publishing is in the defense of its life. Traditional Publishing had filed a suit in your court that Self–Publishing was trying to take over its job and render it entirely irrelevant. One of the prayers of Plaintiff is to ban Self–Publishing from the Space and Network of Publishing to make Traditional Publishing Great Again (TRAPGA).

They made their arguments and presented their cases why they should hold sway in the Publishing Arena. However, the striking argument of Self – Publishing is the fact that the sky is wide enough for every bird to display their flying dexterity. So, how is Self – Publishing now disturbing Traditional Publishers from doing what it knows how to do best?

'It doesn't make sense your honor to ascent to any prayer of Traditional Publishers'.

If you are Judge and the Jury, what will you give us as a verdict?

If I were the Judge, I will give my even-handed verdict as this:

'As long as ample evidence has not been given by Plaintiff that the emergence of Self–Publishing has deterred Traditional Publishing from fulfilling its assignment, I will proceed without much ado to dismiss the litigation of Traditional Publishing as baseless, irrelevant, and repulsive. To this end, the verdict is locked and the decision cannot be appealed in any other court be it of higher or lower jurisdiction'.

'I rest my case.

Self – Publishing is an opportunity that should not be taken lightly by anyone.

What's E-Book Publishing?

An electronic book, also known as an e-book or eBook, is a book publication made available in digital form, consisting of text, images, or both, readable on the flat-panel display of computers or other electronic devices.

If you are a Christian, you will remember the words of the Lord to Marta about her sister Mary, Jesus said 'Mary has chosen the good part of the good one, and it's never going to be taken away from her'.

Interestingly, the good one that Jesus refers to is 'The Word'. This as it were, is inseparable from Publishing.

Remember, in centuries past, before the context of Mary and Marta, the Psalmist had quipped 'God gave the Word, and great is the company of them that published it'.

Civilization as it were, especially Western Civilization wouldn't have been this organized without, inspiration, documentation, Publication, and Preservation.

However, most writers and Authors intend to emerge as a bestseller. Better still, which platform of the two – Traditional Publishers or Self – Publishing – gives an aspiring Writer a shot at becoming a bestselling author?

What is a Bestseller?

A bestseller according to Wikipedia "is a book or other media noted for its top-selling status, with bestseller lists published by newspapers, magazines, and book store chains. Some lists are broken down into classifications and specialties. An author may also be referred to as a bestseller if their work often appears in a list".

However, it is believed that the term 'bestseller' has evolved over the generations.

According to Jeff Goins "Over the years, the term bestseller has carried with it many meanings. At one point, it meant simply a book that sold better than most other books. This was a term that was applied to the works of Charles Dickens, Mark Twain, and Jane Austen. Initially, most bestsellers were primarily works of fiction but over time it began to include more works of nonfiction, including the growing genre of self-help.

Later on, it was considered a pejorative term, suggesting a type of book that was of low literary value. As in, 'there are great works of literature, and then there are... bestsellers."

Bestsellers are usually separated into Fiction and Nonfiction categories. However, compilers have created some other subcategories according to Wikipedia.

But our emphasis is on Amazon's Bestseller List. According to Wikipedia 'Lists from Amazon.com, the dominant online book retailer, are based only on sales from their Web site, and are updated on an hourly basis. Wholesale sales figures are not factored into Amazon's calculations. Numerous Web sites offer advice for authors about a temporary method to boost their book higher on Amazon's list using carefully timed buying campaigns that take advantage of the frequent adjustments to rankings'.

This certifies the importance of the Amazon Publishing Platform because established Publishers rely on its ratings to boost their Author's book sales. This implies that there is no point in traveling far or near if what you are looking for is readily available. Amazon's Kindle Platform is one of the best for stress-free Publishing.

The journey to achieving Bestselling status as an Author is traceable to the notion of your Big Idea, depth of Inspiration, and ability to convey what you are seeing to your readers. This suggests that it is not enough to be inspired, but aspiring Authors must deploy all their inherent capabilities to paint an accurate picture of what lodges in their minds.

Merriam-Webster's definition of a Bestseller settles a lot of issues. It is captioned there as "an article (such as a book) whose sales are among the highest of its class."

Therefore, simply put, a Bestseller is a book whose sale is better than other books. If you want to outsell other Authors, your big idea is your most important selling point.

You are not just regurgitating or rehearsing someone's old idea, but your idea that is meant to shake the world of your readers. If you can give your readers a thought-provoking idea, the seed for the Bestseller is already sown. The best path to becoming a Bestselling Author is the recommendation of your book to your earliest readers.

In this context, you should remember, this other feature that might bring out the best in your piece. What is needed more after starting with a big idea is: writing to your audience in mind. According to Jeff Goins 'Bestsellers are sticky'.

He also suggests that 'you must edit for clarity and not perfection. Bestsellers are clear. You must take out the clutter and ensure your big idea is not lost in the quest of presenting it accurately and simply to your readers.

You must also package the book to spread. Bestsellers are configured to sell. He further said "The title, cover, and design are all optimized to help the message spread. The way people experience your book will affect how well the book sells and how far it spreads. Your goal is to not only get this thing into people's hands; it's to give them something they want to share. This includes the decisions you make regarding title, cover, artwork, and design". Interestingly, Kindle on Amazon has prepared all the tools needed to usher your big idea or inspiration into the pathway of a Bestselling Book.

In conclusion, Jeff Goins who is a Bestselling Author of Five Books counsels us to never stop launching. He avers 'Bestsellers are perennial. The bestselling books of all time typically didn't come out the gates as immediate successes. But because of their timeless nature, they just kept selling. Book launches are great, but you're going to need more than one big event to sell this thing'.

As we prepare to examine the simplicity of the Amazon Kindle, I want to reiterate the fact that the emphasis should always be on the message and not just emerging as a Bestselling Author only. Now if you make it to be one, that's all fine and good. But we must commit to getting timeless truth and changeless counsel out there to instruct and impact the generation that is coming after us in truth and indeed.

CHAPTER 4
PUBLISHING ON AMAZON KINDLE

We have established before now that publishing on Amazon Kindle is not rocket science. It is easy, comprehensive, and beneficial. It is direct, unambiguous, and explicit. If you play your part of creativity assiduously and industriously, the platform gives you an implausible opportunity to launch your big idea on a certified stage globally. You might never know how far your work will go and the depth of influence it could confer.

The steps to take are outlined and explained in the subsequent paragraphs. The steps are plain and self–explanatory. They are not mystifying, just follow the steps and publish your bright ideas for the world to benefit from. You can also smile at the bank as well. We are on a mission to demystify Self-Publishing, on Amazon Kindle.

KDP Formatting Guide using Microsoft Word

There are other means of preparing your document for upload on KDP however if you're needing to, in any case, do it without anyone else's help and do it in Microsoft Word, then, at that point, you'll have the option to design it appropriately involving the means in this guide.

Configuration your book record utilizing Microsoft Word

Assuming you're a writer or author, odds are good that you're as of now acquainted with utilizing Word. Assuming you're an example of the rare type of person that has never utilized Word, that is fine. There is certainly not a precarious expectation to learn and adapt to utilizing the program and you can utilize Word instructional exercise recordings to get the substance.

Organizing your book in Word for Kindle is truly simple. Even though there are specialized viewpoints that you ought to know about, it's truly not excessively complicated.

You can apply designing according to the specialized necessities of the Kindle gadget, which is determined by KDP itself. What's more, frankly, these are not perplexing at all.

At the point when I express arranging for the Kindle is specialized, I mean there are explicit ways that you can do specific things and there are highlights you can't utilize.

For instance, you can't have text enclosing your digital book record, as additionally headers and footers are not permitted on the Kindle device.

How to configure your document for KDP

If you intend to publish on Amazon's KDP, your book's structure should be designed for the KDP Platform. In any case, certain blunders or design issues will happen.

Formatting your Word Document is not the only job needed but you will likewise have to make a unique cover picture.

Employ these requirements for your cover picture while designing your document for Amazon's KDP: the cover picture size ought to be at least 625 pixels on the briefest side and 1000 pixels on the longest side. The top quality ideally is 2,560 x 1,600 pixels as it were.

The recommended file should be a TIFF or JPEG.

Amazon makes it easier by making the Kindle Create Tool accessible to Authors. You can format your Word Document to comply readily with Kindle Standard thereby creating a (.kpf) that can be uploaded on the platform for appraisal, verification, and authentication.

Assuming that there are issues with your Word document when you see it in Kindle Create, you could correct it in Word, and afterward see it preview it again.

Suitable Kindle styles include the following: Indentations, Bold and italics, and Headings.

Limited usage or outright ban of the Word Document features should be noted: Tables, Text boxes, Bullets, Auto Numbering, Special fonts, Headers and footers, and Special Word styles.

Even though you can transfer your Word document outrightly to KDP, I profoundly propose you convert your Word Document to a (.kpf) record before transferring it. A (.kpf) document is Kindle Create's File Extension. This implies it enhances text styles, line dividing, edges, and so on, to further develop poring over your digital book on the Kindle's devices.

#4 - Construction of your book for KDP

A significant stage in distributing your book record to KDP is ensuring you have all the important front and back issues organized for your book.

On the off chance that you don't have the important parts, make certain to add a page in your original copy's Statement document to make the page in your book.

The Five (5) sections to remember for your book structure for KDP are: Cover sheet, Copyright page, Chapter by chapter list, The Body (Your genuine book content), and Back End (Affirmations, Record, Promotion for more Books, and so on).

KDP's Title Page:

This will be followed by a Copyright Page

Something like this:

Copyright © [Year] [Author Name]

Protected by copyright law.

You can also do something like this on the premise of your preference:

Convert your Chapter-by-chapter list for KDP

Employing Kindle's auto ToC instrument will work fine and dandy when you prepare your book's design to distribute on KDP.

Kindle Create automate your ToC passages over completely to hyperlinks as a feature of making a ToC page in your digital book:

#1 - Spot your mouse cursor toward the start of your composition, after the Cover sheet, or Copyright page (if you don't have a clear page after the Cover sheet, add one for the ToC).

#2 - Tap the References tab.

#3 - Move to the Chapter by chapter list button and tap the down key.

#4 - On the drop-down menu, drop your pointer down and tap the Supplement List of the chapter's choice.

#5 - For Macintosh users: Pick the Custom List of chapters' choice.

#6 - On the List of chapters window, uncheck the Show page numbers and look at the box. Since the Kindle device doesn't show page numbers, this isn't needed.

#7 - Tap the Utilization hyperlinks rather than page numbers to take a look at the box.

NOTE: This choice is available in Word for Macintosh, version 16 as it were. Assuming you convert your Word document to Kindle Create, this will be done naturally.

#8 - Add a discretionary Commitment Page

Assuming that you decide to, you can add a devotion page, and that will follow your Chapter by chapter guide.

#9 - Incorporate the body

After the front matter pages, you will have your book's body pages. This incorporates your book's all are satisfied, separated into parts.

The body of your book will ordinarily incorporate the accompanying:

Introduction (fiction), or Prelude (non-fiction)

Chapters or Sections

#10 – How to align your page breaks

Continuously embed a page break toward the end of a part so the new section will begin on another page. Not in the least does this make your book arranging look perfect and harmonized to every reader.

This is the way to embed a page break:

#1 - Place your pointer where you need the break.

#2 - Align the Addition tab, then, at that point, click Page Break.

#3 - You can utilize Ctrl+Enter (Cmd+Enter for Macintosh clients) to embed a page break.

#4 - Update the Match selection and all your part titles will align with this style all through your Word document.

#5 - Using the Heading 1 styles for the section titles in your book will show in your Chapter by chapter list (ToC) so the readers could peruse your digital book.

#6 - Make sure to embed a page break after the last sentence of every part.

#1 – How to Convert your Word document with Kindle Create

When your book's Word document is appropriately organized and all set, you can change over the Word Document using Kindle Create.

Download and install Kindle Create for Windows and macOS.

Click the button indicating Continue.

Pick the sections you want to be included in your Kindle digital book (these will show in your Chapter to chapter guide), by checking or unchecking the Select boxes on the Recommended Part Titles window.

Tap the Acknowledge Chosen button when you are done.

On the left-hand Items nav bar, you can rapidly move to the significant segment (section) in your digital book, by tapping on the important thumbnail.

On the right-hand Text Properties nav bar, you can pick different formatting components to use in your digital book.

NOTE: *Contingent upon the component you pick, the accompanying message will show at the lower part of the Message Properties region: "Tables, Separator, Commentaries, Inline Pictures, and Records can't be altered or arranged in Kindle Create yet."*

Assuming that there are any mistakes with any of the aforesaid, they should be fixed in your Word document, and you will then, at that point, need to upload the document back to Kindle Create.

You can preview the chapters you want to include in your Kindle eBook.

Click the Review button (upper right of the window).

Note the Preview window on the left...

On the Controller, you can change the gadget you need to see your digital book in. The choices are:

   i.   Tablet (Portrait and Landscape)
  ii.   Phone
 iii.   Kindle E-Reader

You can now explore through your digital book to see what it will resemble on the various devices.

You can pick a subject for your digital book, on the Topic choice (right-hand nav bar). After you have picked the subject, click the Select button.

You likewise have the choice to add exceptional components to parts of your digital book, utilizing the Normal Components in the document.

When you're contented with the vibe of your digital book, you can distribute it. However, this doesn't publish your digital book to Kindle Direct Publishing, yet makes the .kpf document and you can transfer that document to KDP, rather than your Word Document.

When you click the Publish button, and your Document has not been saved, an update window will show that your document has not yet been saved. Click the Okay button on this window to initially save your document.

After your record is saved, once more, click the Publish Button (upper right).

Pick where you need to save your .kpf Document, and afterward click the Save button.

Your saved Document will now be accessible to transfer to KDP.

Get ready to independently publish your book on KDP

When your document is appropriately designed and changed over, you can independently publish your book to KDP. Before you open the Encourage Direct Distributing site, be certain you have every one of the vital documents and data expected to finish the cycle.

Checklist to independently publish your digital book on Amazon KDP:

- Completed Word Document on .kpf or otherwise.
- Book title and caption (if you have a caption)
- Non-negotiable quality cover picture (2,813 x 4,500 pixels)
- Your book summary (4,000 characters or less, including spaces)
- Know the class or genre for your book
- Keywords (decide up to seven); twofold phrases are rated as one word for example self-explanatory is viewed as one keyword.
- Your monetary information regarding Royalties.

Complete the means to independently publish on KDP Distributing

Independently publishing a Kindle digital book on Amazon Direct Publishing is truly simple. It requires a couple of moments to fill in the required data and upload your files. Remarkably, within 12 hours (for English language books), your Kindle eBook will be live in the Amazon Kindle Store verifiably.

(Amazon alludes to these as steps, yet they are more similar to segments, which is the reason we've named them thusly).

Inside each part, there are various advances, which we'll go through.

The eBook Checklist

This segment considers concrete Steps for self-publishing on Kindle Direct Publishing:

- Input Book Details

- Validate Your Publication Rights

- Choose your Target Customers

- Set your preferred Release Options

- Upload or attach your already Created Book Cover

- Upload the eBook's File

- Do a quick overview of your Book

EBook's Rights & Pricing

The second part of publishing your book on KDP is focused on your author rights and the pricing of your book, as well as a few other logistics.

The second section to self-publish on KDP includes these steps:

#1 – Confirm and authenticate your publication regions

#2 – Set your preferred price and royalty

#3 – Kindle Matchbook

#4 – Kindle Book Lending

#5. – Optional – KDP Select Benefits

You can decide if you want to enroll in the KDP Select program after you weigh some of the pros and cons.

What are the benefits of KDP Select?

#1 – You earn higher royalties

#2 – You maximize your book's sales potential

#3 – You can reach a new (wider) audience

Publishing Territories

You can choose to select only certain territories to sell your book in, but permitting readers from all regions is far more profitable.

You can now Click the applicable (Worldwide rights – all territories) radio button.

Congratulations – you're now a self-published author on KDP!

Note: when your Kindle eBook is published on Kindle Direct Publishing, it will take about 12 hours (if your book is in English) to be live in the Kindle store (about 48 hours for non-English books).

After uploading to KDP, you will get an email confirmation of your book's availability in the Kindle Store.

You may now proceed to start optimizing your Amazon Author Central Page if you are interested.

You can also order author copies on KDP following these simple steps:

•	Go to your "Bookshelf" and locate the paperback you want to order.

•	Click on the "Order Author Copies" link in the menu.

- Input copies of the book that you want to order.

- Click the drop-down menu to find the Amazon marketplace closest to your shipping address.

- Click "Proceed to check out."

- Complete your order in your Amazon shopping cart.

- Your book copies will be shipped to you after printing.

You will also follow the same pattern to do the cover for the paperback of the same title. Please note that you might need to create a different cover for the two.

However, you will need to input and edit the Author's data, Book's excerpt, upload the picture, and save the Paperback cover.

These are the few steps this volume covers. I guess publishing on Amazon Kindle has been demystified. This is not the end, but the beginning. Research more, read more, and explore more to make the best use of Amazon's Kindle.

CONCLUSION

Since the emergence of the Amazon Kindle, the platform for the ignition of record-breaking acquisition of wisdom, knowledge, and understanding had been activated. The onus from now on is for every aspiring Writer and Author to arise and do as occasion serves them. There is a book in you. Stay-at-home moms are expectantly waiting for tips on how to cope in a post – Covid world. The unprivileged want to hear and see the practical steps you took to get to that enviable level you are today. The struggling college student wants to read about your success of graduating without scholarships and massive student loans they are configured to struggle with after college.

It's about time we focus on the cogency that is inherent in every message that we carry. There's a lesson you have learned, there's a step you wished you had not taken and you don't want anyone else to repeat because it's a waste. Every writer wants to be a bestselling author like

Shakespeare or Sidney Sheldon not forgetting the legendary Agatha Christie. It is ideal to have high and lofty goals, but they shouldn't be the primary. They should be secondary as it were and if you become a bestseller, we will thank God for that Providence. Therefore, the authenticity and the validation of the message, lessons, and counsel should be our primary concerns. When this is settled, everything will naturally fall into place. The bills will be paid and projects will be completed. After all, is said and done, if you do not get your message out there, who will? Since nothing is holding you now, it's about time you bring the book with you. The journal will never be written like no other. The fiction story or comical work that will never be told like any other. Inspirational books that will engender change in a lot of lives. The set time is now.

Since time immemorial, ideas have always taken the stage readily. However, without mincing words, not every inspired idea made it to the limelight. Big ideas have been lost to obscurity, some in transit and others were poorly documented and preserved. Some were never published and some are forever lost in the memory of the recipient of the big idea. Ideas rule the world, inspiration authorizes the revolutionary steps and these two virtues underlay the wisdom for the birth of epochs.

Let's write and publish! Agents and Publishing Houses no longer hold the aces.

INSPIRATIONAL STORIES OF SELF-PUBLISHED AUTHORS

It is fantastic to find out that the most successful self-published book to date is **E.L. James'** *50 Shades of Grey*. *It was not meant to be that efficacious because it* started as fan-fiction for *Twilight and gradually* became its own thing, and it has sold more than 100 million copies globally in addition to holding the record for "fastest-selling paperback." It stayed on the New York Times Bestseller list for 133 consecutive weeks. That's a feat that is begging to be surpassed.

Andy Weir's *The Martian* started as a blog, where he posted the story of a man abandoned on Mars each part in turn. As Brianne Alphonso makes sense of in Electric Lit, "Since individuals appeared to be pretty into the story, Weir chose to gather the sections and sell it on Amazon for a meager $0.99." But soon after, the book assiduously made the New York Times smash hit outline and would later become a feature film that would star Matt Damon.

Doctor, teacher, and creator **Dr. Deane Waldman** independently published *Our Allies Have Become Our Enemies*, the earliest eBook in quite a while seven-book series "Restoring Care to American Healthcare" with some decent professional help. The outcome was that the digital book turned into an Amazon Smash hit and best seller in the first month after publication.

Albeit the computerized age has made

independently publishing a considerably more famous decision, it is the same old thing. A notable feat was achieved in the early 90s when **James Redfield** independently published *The Celestine Prophecy* in 1992. He was selling duplicates out of the storage compartment of his vehicle before Warner Books ultimately took the book on, and it turned into a notable #1 smash, making Redfield one of the forerunners of self-publishing success.

At the point when **Lindsay Buroker** completed the maiden book in her *Emperor's Edge* series, she would have rather not gone chasing after a specialist, and she was worried that a customary distributor wouldn't care that the book conveniently fit into no one genre. She settled for self-publishing and in a year, she published four eBooks and had the option to transit from her everyday employment and make writing a full-time profession."

Amanda Hocking is a writer of paranormal fiction, Hocking was relatively unknown like most debuting writers, and became a bestselling author after deciding to self-publish on Amazon.
Before her feat, she worked a day job caring for disabled people and a night job writing into the wee hours. She wrote a total of 17 unpublished novels, all of them rejected by publishing companies, before deciding to self-publish. A few days after publishing her debut vampire novel, _My Blood Approves_, she sold nine copies a day. She's now written over 25 novels, which you can see on her website.

Robert Kiyosaki In 1997 chose to dump the all-day hustle and composed his lead book, _Rich Dad, Poor Dad_, which has sold 27 million copies. The monetary guidance and one-of-a-kind point of view in the book (to not express anything of the provocative title) made it the # 1 individual accounting book ever.

His books have now been available for more than 20 years, and readers and researchers alike keep on profiting from monetary counsel not commonly shown in schools or even in business degree programs.

LJ Ross (*Louise Ross*) worked as a legal counselor in London when she thought of her DCI Ryan series, situated in Northern Britain. Her independently published books have sold over 5.5 million duplicates, and 18 of them remarkably made it to the #1 spot on the bestsellers' list.

Her maiden novel, *Holy Island*, hit the market in January 2015 and turned into the #1 hit in the Amazon UK and Australia.

From that point forward, she's diverted down a few proposals from distributing organizations and has achieved overall distinction independently.

Mark Dawson who is Thriller author Dawson had two books customarily distributed before he chose to go the independently publishing course. He concedes his initial two books weren't allowed a very remarkable opportunity to hang out in a cutthroat market.

From that experience and his experience as a legal counselor and working for the entertainment world, he's applied what he figured out to influence and facilitate the sales of many independently published books.

He is the prolific writer of the *John Milton series*, the *Beatrix Rose series*, and the *Soho Noir series*, among others, Dawson makes a six-figure pay as a novelist. He has seen his books reach not a few USA Today Bestseller Lists successfully.

Maria E Cantu Alegre wrote and independently published her most notable book, *The Legacy of Lanico*, in 2019 in the wake of seeing the little portrayal of Latinx writers in the book publishing business. She worked with proficient editors to refine her incredible dream, which has a typical rating of 4.9.

Thankful for the opportunity to set off for college and procure a degree, she worked a desk work when a job change provoked her to open a Word document and begin writing.

She's planned and projected four more books for the series and means to go on with the independently publishing course, expecting to motivate other Latinx creatives with adoration for narrating.

Ashwin Sanghi is one of India's bestselling English fiction writers, Sanghi has written bestselling books, including *The Rozabal Line*, *Chanakya's Chant*, *The Krishna Key*, and others. He's likewise co-created two New York Times top-rated thrill rides with the prominent writer, **James Patterson**.

He's likewise co-created a few genuine titles, writing on nurturing, riches, grades, wellbeing, and karma. Forbes India listed him in their Celebrity 100, and he's won a few esteemed grants for his writing achievements.

Maria E Cantu Alegre composed and independently published her most memorable book, The Tradition of Lanico, in 2019 after seeing the little portrayal of Latinx writers in the distributing business. She worked with proficient editors to refine her amazing dream, which has a typical rating of 4.9.

Thankful for the opportunity to head off to college and procure a degree, she did a desk job and a subsequent job change incited her to open a Word doc and begin creative writing.

She projects four more books for the series and plans to go on with the independently publishing course, wanting to move and influence other Latinx creatives with adoration for narrating.

So Friends, let's write and publish with ease on Amazon Kindle, because it's in you, unleash that big idea!!!